Table of Contents

SWING TRADING 2021

Chapter One

Understanding Swing Trading

Swing trading is a trading approach that tries to catch a swing (or "one move").

The thought is to suffer as "little torment" as conceivable by leaving your trades before the restricting weight comes in.

This implies you'll book your benefits before the market switch and crash your benefits.

Let us take a super quick look at the pros and cons of swing trading. They would be discussed fully in a later chapter.

Pros

1. You need not go through hours before your screen in light of the fact that your trades keep going for a considerable length of time or even weeks

2. It's appropriate for those with an all-day work

3. Less pressure contrasted with day exchanging

Cons

1. You won't have the option to ride patterns

2. You have medium-term chance

Everything looks OK?

At this point, we should proceed onward.

Swing Exchanging Techniques

#1 Stuck in a crate

I will be unique and fascinating names to refer to the swing trading techniques I am about to show you in this section.

This causes you to comprehend the trading technique better, so you realize how to apply it to your trading.

Presently, let me acquaint with you the primary swing trading technique for now.

Stuck in a crate is swing trading within a range market in light of the fact that the market is "trapped" between Support and Resistance (to some degree like a container).

Here's the way it works:

Distinguish a range market

Wait patiently for the price to break beneath Support

In the event that the price breaks underneath Support, at that point sit tight and wait for a solid price dismissal (a nearby above Support)

On the off chance that there's a solid value dismissal, at that point go long on the following candle open

Set your stop loss 1 ATR beneath the candle low and take benefits before Resistance

Presently you may be pondering:

"For what reason would it be a good idea for me to take benefits before Resistance?"

The truth is that as a swing trader, you're searching for "one move" in the market.

So to guarantee a high likelihood of achievement, you need to leave your trades before the selling pressure steps in (which is at Resistance).

Bode well?

Great since we'll be applying this idea to the rest of the swing trading techniques.

#2: Catch the wave

This swing trading technique centers around getting "one move" in an inclining market (like a surfer attempting to get the wave).

The thought here is to enter after the pullback has finished when the pattern is probably going to proceed.

Nonetheless, this doesn't work for a wide range of patterns.

Rather, you need to trade trends that have a more profound pullback on the grounds that there's more "meat" towards the upside.

As a rule, you need to see a pullback in any event towards the 50-period frame moving average (MA) or more profound.

Now, let us figure out how to get the wave with this swing trading technique:

Distinguish a pattern that regards the 50MA

In the event that the market moves toward the moving normal, at that point hang tight at a bullish cost dismissal

In the event that there's a bullish value dismissal, at that point go long on next flame

Set your stop loss 1 ATR beneath the low and take benefits just before the swing high

Presently you may be pondering:

"In any case, why the 50-period frame moving average?"

Going with the 50MA is advisable on the grounds that it's viewed by dealers around the globe so that it could prompt an inevitable outcome.

What's more, as a rule, the 50MA agrees with past Resistance turned Support, which makes it progressively noteworthy.

Presently, it doesn't mean you can't utilize 55, 67, 89, or whatever moving average you pick on the grounds that the idea is what makes a difference.

#3: Fade the move

Presently you're most likely reasoning:

"What's the significance of fade?"

It implies to conflict with.

Fundamentally, you're trading against the momentum (otherwise called counter-trend).

Along these lines, if you're the broker that likes to "conflict with the group," at that point, this trading procedure is for you.

Below are the means by which it works.

Recognize a solid momentum move into Resistance that takes out the past high

Search for a solid cost dismissal as the candle structures a solid bearish close

Go short on the following candle and set your stop loss 1 ATR over the highs

Take benefits before the closest swing low

Presently, you have learned 3 sorts of swing trading systems that work.

Be that as it may, there's one extra important thing that is not secured. This thing is your trade management.

For instance:

Consider the possibility that you enter a trade, and the market didn't hit your stop loss.

Be that as it may, neither has it arrived at your objective profit.

So what would it be a good idea for you to do?

Do you hold the trade?

Do you leave the trade?

Or, on the other hand, do you say some prayers?

All things considered, I'll spread all these and more in the following segment

Step By Step Instructions To Properly Handle Your Trades So You Can Trade With Certainty And Conviction

Presently, with trade management, there are 2 different ways you can go about it. These are passive trade management and dynamic or active management.

I'll clarify.

1. Passive trade management

For this technique, you'll either let the market either hit your stop loss or target benefit — anything between, you'll sit idle.

Preferably, you need to set your stop loss away from the "clamor" of the business sectors and have an objective benefit inside a sensible reach (before key market structure).

Below, ypu will find the pros and cons of it.

Pros:

- Trading is progressively loose as your choices become increasingly "digitized."

Cons:

- You can't leave your trade early despite the fact that the market is giving indications of inversion.

It is conceivable to see a triumphant trade become a full 1R misfortune.

2. Dynamic (active) trading

For this, you'll observe how the market responds and afterward choose whether you need to hold or leave the trade.

Presently, this is significant.

For a functioning way to deal with work, you should deal with your trades on your entrance time period (or higher).

Try not to wrongly manage it on a lower time period since you'll terrify yourself out of a trade on each pullback that happens.

Beneath, you will see the pros and cons of it.

Pros

You can limit your losses as opposed to getting a full 1R loss.

Cons

- Progressively stressful

You may leave your trade too early without giving it enough space to run

In the event that dynamic trade management is for you, at that point, below are two methods you can consider.

Moving Average

This method includes utilizing a moving average marker to trail your stops.

You'll clutch the trade if the cost doesn't break past the moving average.

In the event that it does, at that point, you'll leave the trade.

This system is valuable for swing trading methodologies like Catch the Wave in light of the fact that the moving average will, in general, go about as a unique Support and Resistance in slanting markets.

Past bar high/low

This strategy depends on the past bar high/low to trail your stop loss.

This implies on the off chance that you're short, at that point you'll trail your stop loss utilizing the past bar high.

In the event that the market breaks and closes above it, at that point, you'll leave the trade (and the other way around).

This is what I mean:

This method is helpful for swing trading techniques like Fade the Move on the grounds that the market can rapidly turn around against you.

In this way, you would prefer not to give your trade an excessive amount of space to move around and immediately cut your misfortunes when the market gives indications of inversion.

Some Other Techniques Involved In Swing Trading

Scalping

Scalping is one of the most well-known systems. It includes selling very quickly after a trade gets gainful. The value target is whatever consider that interprets along with "you've profited on this arrangement."

Fading

Fading includes shorting stocks after fast moves upward. This depends on the presumption that first, they are overpurchased, second, early buyers are prepared to start taking profits, and third existing buyers might be scared off. Albeit unsafe, this procedure can be amazingly fulfilling. Here, the value target is when purchasers start stepping in once more.

Every day Pivots

This system includes benefitting from a stock's day by day instability. This is finished by endeavoring to purchase at the low of the day and sell at the high of the day. Here, the value target is essentially at the following indication of an inversion.

Momentum

This technique normally includes exchanging on news discharges or finding solid slanting moves bolstered by high volume. One sort of force dealer will purchase on news discharges and ride a pattern until it shows indications of inversion. The other kind will blur the value flood. Here, the value target is when volume starts to diminish.

Much of the time, you'll need to leave an advantage when there is diminished enthusiasm for the stock, as shown by the Level 2/ECN and volume. The benefit target ought to likewise take into consideration more benefits to be made on winning trades than is lost on losing trades. On the off chance that your stop loss is $0.05 away from your entrance value, your objective ought to be more than $0.05 away.

Much the same as your entrance point, characterize precisely how you will leave your trades before entering them. The leave criteria must be sufficiently explicit to be repeatable and testable.

Swing Trading Upsides and Downsides

Upsides

1. Doesn't need to be your all-day work: Anyone with the information and investment capital can have a go at swing trading. Due to the more drawn out time period (from days to weeks instead of minutes and hours), trades don't need to be continually observed. A swing trader can even keep up a different all-day work (as long as the person isn't checking trading screens constantly at work).

2. Potential for critical benefits: Trades, for the most part, need time to work out, and keeping a trade open for a couple of days or weeks may bring about higher benefits than trading in and out of the same security on various occasions a day.

3. Steady observing not required: The swing trader can ensure those stop losses are set up. While there is a danger of a stop being executed at a horrible value, it beats the steady checking of every vacant position that is an element of day trading.

4. Less pressure and danger of burnout: Since swing trading is only here and there an all-day work, there is substantially less possibility of burnout through pressure. Swing traders, for the most part, have a standard activity or another wellspring of salary from which they can balance or alleviate trading misfortunes.

5. Costly investment not required: Swing trading should be possible with only one PC and traditional trading instruments. It doesn't require the cutting edge innovation of day trading.

Downsides

1. Higher edge prerequisites: Since swing trading, for the most part, includes positions held at any rate medium-term, edge necessities are higher. Most extreme influence is generally multiple times one's capital. Contrast this and day trading where edges are multiple times one's capital.

2. The danger of generous losses: As with any style of trading, swing trading can likewise bring about significant losses. Since swing brokers hold their situations for longer than day traders, they likewise risk bigger losses.

Chapter Two

Earning $15000 Per Month In Stock Trading

The financial trade's normal return is a cool 10% every year — superior to anything you can discover in a ledger or bonds. So what is the reason behind why such a large number of individuals neglect to acquire that 10%, regardless of putting resources into the financial trade? Many don't remain committed long enough.

The way to making cash in stocks is staying in the financial trade; your length of "time in the market" is the best indicator of your complete presentation. Tragically, investors frequently move all through the securities trade even from a pessimistic standpoint potential occasions, passing up that yearly return.

(First of all: You need an investment fund to contribute — and along these lines profit — in the financial trade.

To make cash putting resources into stocks, stay committed

Additional time rises to a greater open door for your investments to go up. The best organizations will in general, increment their benefits after some time, and investors reward this more noteworthy income with a higher stock cost. That more significant expense converts into an arrival for speculators who possess the stock.

Additional time in the market likewise enables you to gather profits, if the organization pays them. In case you're trading in and out of the market on day by day, week after week or month to month premise, you can kiss those profits farewell since you likely won't claim the stock at the basic focuses on the schedule to catch the payouts.

If a market offered about 9.9% returns from 2017 till now, you would make a lot of profit.

Nonetheless, on the off chance that you missed only the 10 greatest days in that period, your yearly return dropped to 5%.

In the event that you missed the 20 greatest days, your yearly return dropped to 2%.

In the event that you missed the 30 greatest days, you really lost cash (- 0.4% yearly).

When the day ends, you would have earned twice as much by staying committed (and you don't need to screen the market, either!) for only 10 extra basic days. Nobody can foresee which days those will be, be that as it may, so investors must remain committed the entire time to catch them.

The more you're in, the closer you'll get to that verifiable normal yearly return of 10%.

Reasons That Prevent You From Making Money Investment

The stock market is the main market where the merchandise goes at a bargain and everybody turns out to be too reluctant to even think about buying. That may sound senseless. However, it's actually what happens when the market plunges even a couple of percent, as it regularly does. Investors become frightened and sell in a frenzy. However, when costs rise, speculators plunge in fast. It's an ideal formula for "purchasing high and selling low."

To evade both of these limits, investors need to comprehend the average untruths they let themselves know. Here are three of the greatest:

1. 'I'll hold up until the financial trade is sheltered to commit.'

This reason is utilized by investors after stocks have declined when they're too reluctant to even think about buying into the market. Possibly stocks have been declining a couple of days straight or maybe they've been on a long haul decay. Be that as it may, when investors state they're sitting tight for it to be protected, they mean they're trusting that costs will climb. So hanging tight for (the impression of) wellbeing is only an approach to wind up following through on greater expenses, and in reality, it is regularly just a view of security that investors are paying for.

What drives this conduct: Fear is the directing feeling, yet therapists call this progressively explicit conduct "nearsighted misfortune repugnance." That is, investors would prefer to maintain a strategic distance from a transient loss at any expense than accomplish a more extended term gain. So when you feel torment at losing cash, you're probably going to stop that loss successfully. So you sell stocks or don't purchase in any event, when costs are modest.

2. 'I'll buy it again when it is lower in a week from now.'

This reason is employed by would-be buyers as they assume that the stock will become lower. However, investors never really know what direction stocks will proceed onward any given day, particularly for the time being. A stock or market could simply go up as well as go down in a week's time. Smart investors purchase stocks when they're modest and hold them after some time.

What drives this conduct: It could be dread or insatiability. The dreadful investor may stress the stock is going to fall this week and pauses, while the insatiable speculator anticipates that a fall yet needs should attempt to improve cost than today's.

3. 'I'm exhausted of this stock, so I'm selling.'

This reason is utilized by investors who need fervor from their ventures, similar to activity in a gambling club. Be that as it may, savvy contributing is really exhausting. The best investors sit on their stocks for a considerable length of time and years, letting them compound additions. Contributing is certainly not a brisk hit game, normally. Every one of the additions come while you pause, not while you're trading in and out of the market.

What drives this conduct: an investor's longing for fervor. That longing might be powered by the misinformed idea that effective financial specialists are exchanging each day to win enormous increases. While a few dealers do effectively do this, even they are savagely and soundly centered around the result. For them, it's not about fervor but instead profiting, so they keep away from emotional decision making.

File Assets Or Individual Stocks?

On the off chance that that 10% yearly return sounds great to you, at that point, the spot to put is in a record subsidize. File reserves contain handfuls or even several stocks that mirror a record, for example, the S&P 500, so you need little information about individual organizations to succeed. The primary driver of accomplishment, once more, is the control to remain contributed.

Truly, you conceivably can win a lot better yields in singular stocks than in bulk stock, yet you'll have to place some perspiration into exploring organizations to procure it.

Instructions to Make Lots of Money in Online Stock Trading

Putting resources into the financial trade can be an incredible method to have your cash profit, especially in the present monetary atmosphere where investment accounts and long haul certified receipts do not give mega returns. Stock trading is definitely not an activity that is devoid of risk, and a few misfortunes are unavoidable. Nonetheless, with quality research and interests in the correct organizations, stock trading can possibly be entirely beneficial.

1. Research ebb and flow patterns. There are numerous trustworthy sources that report on advertise patterns. You may have to purchase a stock-trading magazine, for example, Kiplinger, Investor's Business Daily, Traders World, The Economist, or Bloomberg BusinessWeek.

You could likewise follow online journals composed by effective market experts, for example, Abnormal Returns, Deal Book, Footnoted, Calculated Risk, or Zero Hedge.

2. Pick a trading site. A percentage of the top of the line sites incorporates Scottrade, OptionsHouse, TD Ameritrade, Motif Investing and TradeKing. Be certain that you know about any exchange expenses or rates that will be charged before you settle on a site to utilize.

Be certain the administration you utilize is respectable. You should peruse audits of the business on the web.

Select a help that has benefits, for example, a cell phone application, investor instruction and research apparatuses, low trade charges, simple to understand information, and all day, everyday client assistance.

3. Create an account with at least one trading site. You're probably not going to require multiple, however, you might need to begin with at least two so you can later narrow down your choice to the site that draws you in the most.

Make certain to look at the base necessities for each site. Your monetary limit may just enable you to make accounts on a couple of destinations.

Beginning with an especially modest amount, like $1,000, may restrain you to certain trading platforms, as others have higher least adjusts.

4. Work on trading before you put genuine cash in. A few sites offer a virtual exchanging stage, where you can analyze for some time to evaluate your impulses without placing real cash in. Obviously, you can't profit along these lines, yet you additionally can't lose money.

Trading this way will get you used to the techniques and kinds of choices you will be looked with when trading; however, by and large, it is a poor portrayal of real trading. In genuine trading, there will be a defer when purchasing and selling stocks, which may bring about unexpected costs in comparison to what you were focusing on. Furthermore, trading with virtual cash won't set you up for the pressure of exchanging with your genuine cash.

5. Pick solid stocks. You have a lot of decisions; at the end of the day, it is very important that you buy stock from firms that are

leaders in their specialty, offer packages that people in the stock broking business reliably need, have a stellar and transparent brand image, and have a great plan of action and a proven track record of progress.

Investigate an organization's open budgetary reports to assess how productive they are. A progressively productive organization, as a rule, implies an increasingly beneficial stock. You can discover total money related data about any traded on an open market organization by visiting their site and finding their latest yearly report. In the event that it isn't on the site, you can consider the organization and solicitation a printed version.

Take a look even under the least favorable conditions quarter on record and choose if the danger of rehashing that quarter merits the potential for benefit.

Ensure that you take a careful look into the organization's management, working expenses, and responsibilities. Investigate their monetary record and income declaration and decide whether they are beneficial or have a decent opportunity to be later on.

Analyze the stock history of a particular organization to the presentation of its friend organizations. On the off chance that all innovation stocks were down at a certain point, assessing them comparatively with one another as opposed to the whole market can reveal to you which organization has been over its industry reliably.

Tune in to an organization's profit phone calls. Initially, investigate the organization's quarterly income discharge that is posted online as a public statement about an hour prior to the call.

6. Purchase your first stocks. At the point when you are prepared, dive in, and purchase a few dependable stocks. The careful number will rely upon your spending limit, yet go for in any event two. Organizations that are notable and have built up exchanging narratives and great notorieties are commonly the most steady stocks and a decent spot to begin. Start exchanging little and utilize a measure of money you are set up to lose.

It is sensible for an investor to start trading with as little as $1,000. You simply must be careful so as to maintain a strategic distance from enormous trade expenses, as these can without much of a stretch gobble up your benefits when you have a little record balance.

7. Put generally in mid-top and huge top organizations. Mid-top firms are those that have a market valuation somewhere in the range of two and $10 billion. Huge top organizations have market valuations bigger than $10 billion, while those with market tops littler than $2 billion are little tops.

Market capitalization is determined by increasing an organization's stock cost by the number of offers exceptional.

8. Screen the business sectors every day. Recollect the cardinal guideline in stock trading is to purchase low and sell high. In the event that your stock worth has expanded, essentially, you might need to assess whether you should sell the stock and reinvest the benefits in other (lower evaluated) stocks.

9. Think about putting resources into shared assets. Shared assets are effectively dealt with by an expert director and incorporate a mix of stocks. These will be expanded with interests in such areas as innovation, retail, money related, vitality, or remote organizations.

1. Purchase low. This implies when stocks are at a moderately low value dependent on the previous history, you get them. Obviously, nobody knows for sure when the costs will go up or down—that is the test in stock contributing.

To decide whether a stock is undervalued, take a careful look at the firm's income per share just as obtaining movement by organization representatives. Search for organizations, specifically businesses and markets where there are bunches of instability, as that is the place you can rake in boatloads of cash.

2. Sell high. You need to sell your stocks when they are at their height dependent on the previous history. On the off chance that you sell the stocks for more cash than you got them for, you profit. The greater the growth from when you got them to when you sold them, the more cash you make.

3. Try not to sell in a frenzy. When you notice a stock you have drops lower than the value you got it for, your sense might be to dispose of it. While there is a chance that it can continue falling and never rise back up, you ought to think about how probable it is that it might

bounce back. Selling for loss is not generally the best thought since you lock in your loss.

4. Concentrate on the basic and specialized market investigation strategies. These are the two very important models of understanding the financial exchange and looking at value changes. The model you use will determine how you settle on choices about what stocks to purchase and when to purchase and sell them.

A principal examination settles on choices about an organization dependent on what they do, their character and notoriety, and who drives the organization. This examination looks to give a real incentive to the organization and, by expansion, the stock.

A specialized investigation takes a gander at the whole market and what inspires investors to purchase and sell stocks. This includes inspecting patterns and breaking down speculator responses to occasions.

Numerous financial specialists utilize a blend of these two strategies to settle on educated venture choices.

5. Think about putting resources into organizations that deliver profits. A few investors, known as career investors, want to put as a rule in profit paying stocks. This is a way that your stock can make money regardless of whether they don't value the cost. Profits are organization benefits paid straightforwardly to investors quarterly. Regardless of whether you choose to put resources into these stocks will depend altogether on your own objectives as a speculator.

Building up Your Stock Portfolio

1. Differentiate your property. When you have set up some stock property, and you have discovered how buying and selling works to some extent, you ought to grow your stock portfolio. This means that you should invest your money in a wide range of stocks.

New firms may be a decent choice after you have a foundation of more established firm stock built up. In the event that a startup is purchased by a greater organization, you might rake in boatloads of cash rapidly. Notwithstanding, know that 90% of new businesses last less than 5 years, which makes them risky ventures.

Think about investigating various businesses also. On the off chance that your unique property is for the most part, in innovation organizations, take a stab at investigating assembling or retail. This will differentiate your portfolio against negative industry patterns.

2. Reinvest your cash. At the point when you sell your stock (ideally for much more than you got it for), you should fold your cash and benefits into purchasing new stocks. On the off chance that you can profit each day or consistently, you're en route to securities trade achievement.

Consider placing a segment of your benefits into reserve funds or retirement account.

3. Put resources into an IPO (initial public offering). An IPO is the first list an organization issues stock. This can be an incredible time to purchase stock in an organization you accept will be fruitful, as the IPO offering cost frequently (yet not generally) ends up being the least value ever for an organization's stock.

4. Go out on a limb when making a decision on stocks. The ideal way to rake in boatloads of cash in the securities exchange is to go for broke and get somewhat fortunate. This does not mean that you should stake everything on unsafe ventures and trust in the best, however. Contributing ought not to be played a similar route as betting. You should look into each investment altogether and be certain that you can recoup monetarily if your exchange goes inadequately.

On the one hand, avoiding any and all risks with just settled stocks won't typically enable you to "beat the market" and increase exceptionally significant yields. In any case, those stocks will, in general, be steady, which implies you have a lower possibility of losing cash. What's more, with relentless profit installments and representing a risk, these organizations can wind up being a greatly improved investment than less secure organizations.

You can likewise decrease your risk by supporting against losses on your investments. Perceive how to fence in ventures for more data.

5. Be mindful of the draw back of day trading. Financier firms will as a rule charge expenses for each exchange that can truly add. If you make way more than a specific number of trades every week, the Security Exchange Commission insists that you have to set up a company account with a high least equalization. Day trading is known for losing individuals' bunches of cash just as being unpleasant, so it is generally better to contribute over a significant stretch of time.

6. Converse with a Certified Public Accountant (CPA). When you start profiting in the securities trade, you might need to converse with a bookkeeper about how your benefits will be burdened. All things considered, while it's in every case best to converse with an expense proficient, by and large, you will have the option to sufficiently examine this data for yourself and abstain from paying an expert.

7. Realize when to get out. Trading the securities trade resembles legitimate betting and not a fair interest in the long haul time frame. This is the area where it is not the same as investing, which is longer-term and more secure. A few people can build up an

unfortunate fixation on exchanging, which can lead you to lose a great deal (even the entirety) of your cash. In the event that you have an inclination that you're losing control of your capacity to profit, attempt to discover help before you lose everything. In the event that you see an expert who is keen, judicious, objective and dispassionate, approach that individual for help if you feel overwhelmed.

Chapter Three

Risk Management in Stock Trading

We should truly go out on a limb look at what risk is. Risk is the plausibility of loss or damage, something that appears to be risky to us. Risk is questionable; it is capricious. At the point when you characterize trading risk, you are computing the likelihood of a stock going up versus that of it going down. This is valuable since it enables you to gauge how a lot of trading risks you are eager to take against the probability of an increase considering the vulnerability. It is fundamental to be happy to accept trading risk orders to accomplish the ideal consequence of profits.

In stock trading, there is a solid connection between risk and reward: more prominent the risk, the more prominent the income for the most part. In monetary wording, risk management is the way toward distinguishing and evaluating the risk and afterward creating systems to oversee and limit the equivalent while expanding the profits.

Each investment requires a specific measure of risk, and for an investor to expect this risk, he must be remunerated properly. This pay is through something many refer to as the risk premium or basically the premium. Risk is thusly key to stock trading or investment in light of the fact that without risk, there can be no gains. Effective traders utilize stock trading risk management techniques to limit the risk and expand the gain.

In stock markets, there are commonly two kinds of risks; first, the Market risk and second the Inflation risk. Market risk results from a plausibility in increment or decline of financial markets. The other risk which is Inflation or purchasing power risks, results from the rise and fall of costs of merchandise and ventures after some time.

The inflation risk is a significant thought in long haul investments, whereas the market risk is increasingly applicable for the time being. It is the market risk that can be overseen and controlled somewhat; inflation risk can't be controlled.

What Is An Appropriate Level Of Risk?

It is troublesome now and again to draw a line between reasonable risk and negligent risk. This will require significant practice, ideally through paper trading. Additionally, you should work at increasing a superior comprehension of the organization you are managing by performing principal examination and specialized investigation, lastly, control your very own mental commitment to the procedure.

On the off chance that you are too risk unwilling, or "trading terrified," you won't have the stomach to hold your triumphant positions sufficiently long to understand the potential benefits that you anticipate. On the other hand, if you are an activity addict and risk excessively, you may get into a round of taking gigantic drawdowns and that can mentally wear on your mind over the trading day. With focus, you can figure out how to endure the vulnerability and brave the awkward inclination that a drawdown presents. After some time, you will start to trade the "zone," a mentality of activity, concentrating on the present time and place, without harping on your past errors or feelings. This will enable you to go out on a limb, equalization and size your trading risk, and endure the questionable idea of the risk.

There are sure systems that can be utilized to alleviate the risk in a stock exchange. The systems are as per the following:

-Defining Goals

An incredible way to handle the vulnerability in the business sectors is to define future situated objectives for yourself and afterward build up an exchanging methodology or exchanging framework that will enable you to accomplish that outcome. It is basic that you remain lined up with your objectives and exchanging procedures; by doing this, you help to take out a portion of the vulnerability and make the risk progressively sensible and perceptible.

-Know Who You Are As A Trader

In the event that you can connect with your center being, you would then be able to shape your trading with no previously established inclinations by any stretch of the imagination. That is the way to progress, to be fluid and change in accordance with various market situations without the conscience and the hard cap.

Numerous dealers state that the brain research of risk is the brain research of certainty. Certainty implies realizing how to trade all circumstances, and this accompanies practice and tolerance. On the off chance that you get that feeling in your gut that you are "betting," you are most likely not certain. Certainty originates from dependable predictable increases. Be calm and pursue your trading plan and certainty will normally come. In your center, you realize that up to 14 days of additions don't make you an expert. Be straightforward with yourself.

-Figure out how to Trade Stocks, Futures, and ETFs Risk-Free

Going out on a limb and vanquishing market vulnerability expects you to be on the bleeding edge, adapting new abilities, and adhere to your exchanging plan even despite the trouble. Drop your self-image, enable yourself to be instructed by others with experience. Try not to be reluctant to ask questions and don't want to be in charge constantly. The best merchants that I have seen are modest, strong, and continually hoping to better their exchanging aptitudes with the goal that they can remain grounded and objective in taking care of their risk.

Also, going out on a limb and disposing of the market vulnerability requires a merchant to take a shot at not getting diverted, augmentative, or even excessively stubborn. Have the option to get littler in trade size when your trades are conflicting with you. Try not to enable your sense of self to assume a major job in your trading exercises by holding losing positions route longer than you ought to be, gambling fiasco. Be fluid and enable yourself to build your range of abilities and adopt new ideas.

-Follow the pattern of the market

This is one of the demonstrated strategies to limit risks in a stock trade. The issue is that it is hard to spot slants in the market and patterns change extremely quick. A market pattern may last a solitary day, a month or a year, and again, transient patterns work inside long haul patterns.

-Portfolio Diversification

Another helpful risk management methodology in the stock market is to broaden your risk by putting resources into a portfolio. In a portfolio, you enhance your venture to a few organizations, parts and resource classes. There is a likelihood that while the market estimation of a specific venture diminishes, that of the other may increase. Mutual Funds are one more way to enhance the effect.

-Stop Loss

Stop-loss or trailing apparatus is one more tool to watch that you don't lose cash should the stock go far a fall. In this procedure, the trader has the choice of making an exit if a specific stock falls beneath a specific determined breaking point. Self-restraint is one more alternative utilized by certain investors to sell when the stock falls underneath a specific level or when there is a lofty fall.

-Proper Risk Management

Ask Warren Buffett, the best financial specialist ever, what is your recommendation to investors, and he says, "don't lose money." But stock market hints risk and luckily, there are sufficient methodologies for a shrewd financial specialist to protect his cash and guarantee gain. A cautious and auspicious exercise of these alternatives causes you to see the risk in question.

Risk management assists with bringing down losses. It can likewise help shield a trader's account from losing the entirety of their money. The risk happens when the dealer endures a loss. On the off chance that it needs to be handled, the broker can open oneself up to profiting in the market.

It is a basic yet regularly disregarded essential to fruitful dynamic trading. All things considered, a trader who has produced generous benefits can lose it all in only a couple of terrible trades without an appropriate risk management system. So how would you build up the best systems to control the dangers of the market?

This part will talk about some straightforward techniques that can be utilized to ensure your exchanging benefits.

-Arranging Your Trades

As Chinese military general Sun Tzu's broadly stated: "Each fight is won before it is fought." This expression suggests that arranging and technique—not the fights—win wars. Additionally, fruitful brokers regularly quote the expression: "Trade the exchange and trade the plan." Just like in war, preparing can frequently mean the difference between progress and disappointment.

To begin with, ensure your trader is right for frequent trading. A few traders take into account clients who trade inconsistently. They charge high commissions and don't offer the privilege of logical tools for dynamic traders.

Stop-loss (S/L) and take-benefit (T/P) focuses speak to two key manners by which traders can prepare when trading. Effective traders recognize what value they are eager to follow through on and at what cost they are happy to sell. They would then be able to gauge the subsequent returns against the likelihood of the stock hitting their objectives. If the balanced return is sufficiently high, they execute the exchange.

Then again, fruitless traders frequently enter a trade without having any thought of the points at which they will sell at a benefit or a misfortune. Like players on a fortunate—or unfortunate streak—feelings start to dominate and direct their traders. Losses regularly incite individuals to hang on and would like to make their cash back, while benefits can lure traders into hanging on for considerably more gains incautiously.

I find that you can ask yourself a couple of inquiries to keep yourself grounded and better comprehend your trading plan. Think about a couple of ongoing trades that you made, audit the stock chart, and ask yourself the accompanying:

- What cost did you enter the trade?

- Did you include extra offers as the stock went in support of you?

- Where did you sell out?

- Would you be able to associate your trading style with the way in which you dealt with the trade?

- Did you purchase stocks close to the base and afterward include more as the stock went up? Or on the other hand, did you purchase and sold rapidly once you handled a little profit?

- What lessons would you be able to find out about your trading style from the manner in which you dealt with this trade?

- How might others have traded this stock chart? What do you have to do so as to develop your trading style and the measure of risk you are happy to expect?

- What is keeping you away from doing this?

- What is a staying point for you that is counteracting you to arrive at that next level, something that you experience difficulty with in light of the fact that it creates a lot of uneasiness and vulnerability?

- Do you experience difficulty purchasing/shorting more offers in any event, when you are extremely certain that you are correct? This line of addressing should assist you with understanding who you are as a broker and what steps you have to go out on a limb to improve your trading risk profile.

-Consider the One-Percent Rule

A lot of day traders pursue what's known as the one-percent rule. Essentially, this dependable guideline proposes that you should never put over 1% of your capital or your trading account into a solitary trade. So in the event that you have $10,000 in your exchanging account, your situation in some random instrument shouldn't be more than $100.

This system is regular for traders who have records of under $100,000—some even go as high as 2% in the event that they can manage the cost of it. Numerous brokers whose accounts have higher limits may decide to go with a lower rate. That is on the

53

grounds that as the size of your account increases, so too does the position. The ideal approach to hold your losses under wraps is to keep the standard underneath 2%—any more and you'd chance a considerable measure of your trading account.

-Setting Stop-Loss and Take-Profit Points

A stop-loss point is a cost at which a broker will sell a stock and write off the trade. This regularly happens when a trade doesn't work out the manner in which a broker trusted. The focuses are intended to forestall the "it will return" mindset and cutoff losses before they raise. For instance, if a stock breaks underneath a key help level, traders regularly sell at the earliest opportunity.

Then again, a take-profit point is the cost at which a dealer will sell a stock and take a profit on the trade. This is the point at which the extra upside is constrained, given the risks. For example, if a stock is moving toward a key opposition level after an enormous move upward, traders might need to sell before the time of solidification happens.

The ideal approach to predefine the risk you are eager to take is to construct a stop loss management plan. Above all else, each time you are entering a trade, you have to have a stop loss so as to secure your bankroll. At the point when you are taking a shot at your trading procedure, you ought to distinguish the level of the trade size you are happy to hazard. At the point when you discover this rate, you ought to do a basic count so as to characterize the level at which your stop misfortune ought to be set.

Suppose your bankroll is $10,000. As such, after the most extreme day trading leverage of 1:4, you will have a purchasing power of $40,000. Presently suppose that the greatest risk you are eager to take rises to 1% of your bankroll. This implies you are prepared to chance 10,000 x 0.01 = $100 most extreme in every one of your trades. In any case, the purchasing power you are overseeing is $40,000, isn't that so?

Presently you have to characterize the amount of your purchasing power. You are eager to put resources into every one of your trades. Suppose you need to invest 1/8 of your purchasing power ($40,000) in every one of your trades. This implies you will put 40,000 x 1/8 = $5,000 in every one of your arrangements. We will risk $100 (1% of the account) in each trade with contributing $5,000. So as to discover the correct area of your stop loss, you have to characterize what rate $100 take from $5,000. We can find this out with a basic calculation:

100/5,000 = 2% (0.02)

As such, your stop loss ought to consistently be at a 2% good ways from the passage cost. Along these lines, you will consistently risk $100, which is 1% of your bankroll.

Instructions to More Effectively Set Stop-Loss Points

Setting stop-loss and take-profit points are frequently done utilizing technical analysis, yet principal analysis can likewise assume a key job in timing. For instance, if a trader is holding stock in front of earnings as fervor builds, the person might need to sell before the news hits the market if desires have gotten excessively high, paying little heed to whether the take-profit price has been hit.

Moving averages speak to the most well-known approach to set these points, as they are anything but difficult to ascertain and generally followed by the market. Key moving averages incorporate the 5-, 9-, 20-, 50-, 100-and 200-day averages. These are best set by applying them to a stock's chart and seeing if the stock price has responded to them in the past as either a help or obstruction level.

Another extraordinary method to put stop-loss or take-profit points is on help or opposition pattern lines. These can be drawn by interfacing past highs or lows that happened on critical, better than expected volume. Like with moving averages, the key is deciding points at which the value responds to the pattern lines and, obviously, on high volume.

When setting these focuses, here are some key contemplations:

- Utilize longer-term moving averages for increasingly unpredictable stocks to diminish the opportunity that an insignificant cost swing will trigger a stop-loss request to be executed.

- Alter the moving averages to coordinate objective value ranges. For instance, longer targets should utilize bigger moving averages to decrease the quantity of sign created.

- Stop losses ought not to be nearer than 1.5-times the present high-to-low range (unpredictability), as it is too liable to even think about getting executed without reason.

- Alter the stop loss as per the market's unpredictability. In the event that the stock cost isn't moving excessively, at that point, the stop-misfortune focuses can be fixed.

- Utilize referred to crucial occasions, for example, profit discharges, as key timeframes to be in or out of a trade as instability and vulnerability can rise.

-Reward-to-Risk Ratio (Win-Loss)

In each trade you attempt, you ought to have plainly expressed objectives. This implies you ought to consistently realize the amount you are prepared to lose and what you are focusing on as far as a profit target. However, how would you do that? Simple! A similar route likewise with stop loss management. Be that as it may, this time you deal with your objective.

On the off chance that you focus on benefit equivalent to 1% of your bankroll, you should get a 2% expansion. Along these lines, you will risk 1% of your bankroll (2% of the exchange) and you will focus on 1% benefit (2% expansion). For this situation, you have 1:1 Return-to-Risk proportion, since you hazard 1 to get 1.

1:1 is the base you should focus on if you execute high reoccurrence trading and you open more than one exchange for every day. At the end of the day, don't chance more than you focus on in the event that you are a day trader.

Be that as it may, there is an exemption. In the event that you actualize a high likelihood technique, where the achievement rate is more than 65-70%, at that point, you can put a free stop loss. The purpose behind this is the stop might be intended to shield you from quick value moves against your exchange. The free stop loss could likewise be utilized when you leave your exchanges medium-term (which I don't advise).

Now and again, when you need to trade a major loop, you can extricate your stop loss so as to adapt to amazingly high instability during the opening chime.

Just to explain something on the stop loss, you don't need to enable your order to be activated. In the event that I am searching for a particular increase of supposing 2% and the stock starts to come up short, I will utilize time and deals to pass judgment on the off chance that I should leave an exchange.

Along these lines, after some time, your success proportion will keep on expanding which, will build your per normal exchange benefit. It will likewise put you in a champ's attitude as you get in a steady musicality of hauling cash out of the market.

-Computing Expected Return

Setting stop-loss and take-profit points are additionally important to compute the normal return. The significance of this computation can't be exaggerated, as it powers traders to consider their trades and support them thoroughly. Also, it gives them a precise method to look at different trades and select just the most beneficial ones.

This can be determined utilizing the accompanying formula:

[(Probability of Gain) x (Take Profit % Gain)] + [(Probability of Loss) x (Stop-Loss % Loss)]

The result of this calculation is a normal return for the dynamic broker, who will, at that point, measure it against different risks to figure out which stocks to trade. The likelihood of gain or loss can be determined by utilizing authentic breakouts and breakdowns from the help or obstruction levels—or for experienced brokers, by making an informed investment.

-Trailing Stop Loss Order (TSLO)

Profits will run in support of you to a point, and afterward, out of the blue, things can conflict with you rapidly.

In the event that you are in a trade and the value moves in support of you, there is nothing amiss with altering your stop. Along these lines, you can secure ensured benefits.

The trailing stop is a customary on-chart market order, which gets you out of the trade when explicit prerequisites are met. As you presumably surmise, the name "trailing stop" is connected with the character of the request. The trailing stop essentially trails behind the value activity, when the stock is inclining toward you. Be that as it may, if the stock is moving against you, the trailing stop doesn't move.

Assume you purchase Oracle at $35.00 per offer, and you place a trailing stop at $0.35 (35 pennies) underneath your entrance cost.

This implies your trailing stop will get you out of the market at $34.65 if the value diminishes right away.

Notwithstanding, if ORCL enters a bullish pattern and the cost increases to $36.00 per share, at that point, the trailing stop will be consequently balanced at $35.65 per share. Since we entered at $35.00, we will have a secured benefit of $0.65 (65 pennies).

If, in the wake of coming to $36.00 per share, the value starts to drop, the trailing stop holds at $35.65. On the other hand, if the value starts to transcend $36, the trailing stop misfortune will move higher as needs are.

A key thing to recall when putting trailing stops is to account for the instability of the hidden security. This means if a stock has 3% moves per light, a .5% trailing stop will be activated.

-Differentiate and Hedge

Ensuring you capitalize on your trading implies never placing your eggs in a single basket. In the event that you put all your cash in one stock or one instrument, you're setting yourself up for a major loss. So make sure to differentiate your investments—crosswise over both industry part just as market capitalization and geographic area. In addition to the fact that this helps you deal with your risk, however, it additionally opens you up to more chances.

You may likewise get yourself when you have to support your position. Consider a stock position when the outcomes are expected. You may think about taking the contrary situation through options, which can help ensure your position. When trading action dies down, you would then be able to loosen up the fence.

-Downside Put Options

If you are endorsed for options trading, purchasing a downside put option, once in a while known as a protective put, can likewise be utilized as support to stem losses from a trade that goes bad. A put option gives you the right; however, not the investment, to sell the fundamental stock at a predetermined value evaluated at or before the alternative lapses. Subsequently in the event that you possess XYZ stock from $100 and purchase the half-year $80 put for $1.00 per alternative in premium, at that point, you will be successfully halted out from any value dip under $79 ($80 strike less the $1 premium paid).

The Bottom Line

Traders ought to consistently know when they intend to enter or leave a trade before they execute. By utilizing stop losses viably, a trader can limit misfortunes as well as the occasions an exchange is left unnecessarily. Taking everything into account, make your fight arrangement early, so you'll definitely realize you've won the war.

Chapter Four

Time Management In Stock Trading

There are numerous advantages to being a broker. One of the fundamental reasons we love being a broker is about adaptability. This implies we don't need to get up right on time to get down to business, we don't have a supervisor to instruct us, we can take getaways at whatever point we need and we can likewise control our very own time.

Numerous traders anyway have a test in dealing with their time, since they don't have the foggiest idea how to oversee it in a compelling way. In this chapter, we will feature a couple of approaches to deal with your time successfully as a broker.

1. A decent rest

A few people like to boast about sleeping for a few hours. 'I will rest soundly when I bite the dust,' they say.

Donald Trump, the United States president, has consistently boasted about how he sleeps for three hours consistently. He contends that it is hard for an individual that sleeps for 8 hours to rival one who rests for 3 hours.

About this, I have an alternate opinion.

I have faith in having a decent night's rest. Rest causes you to remain invigorated during the day. It additionally encourages you to maintain a strategic distance from the burnout that has affected such a large number of individuals. The ideal approach to deal with rest is to rest early and afterward get up right on time also.

2. Have objectives

One of the fundamental reasons why a great many people don't accomplish their time management goals is that they don't have objectives. Having objectives implies having a lot of things that you need to accomplish inside a specific timeframe. Without objectives, you will have a test of time management.

For example, each morning, you need to have a list of things that you need to accomplish during the day. At the point when you have this arrangement of things, you will be in a decent position to accomplish most during a brief timeframe.

3. Organize

You ought to figure out how to organize your undertakings. This implies you ought to consistently attempt to do the most significant things first. For example, if your primary occupation is trading, you ought to do the best to attempt to do or plan your trading early in the morning. This is the place you ought to invest a ton of energy.

Set aside some effort to peruse, watch, and do your trading tasks first. By doing this, you will be in a decent position to make progress. You ought to abstain from trading when you are drained or when you have a great deal going on.

4. Go on breaks

The issue with numerous individuals is that they need to seem occupied. In any event, when they do not have anything to do, you will see them attempt to accomplish something. The test with this is efficiency is exceptionally diminished.

As a broker, you ought to consistently concentrate on profitability. You ought to be content on each one hour spent well. Hence, in your trading day, you ought to have breaks.

5. Stay away from interruptions

Finally, you ought to give a valiant effort to evade interruptions. This is a zone where numerous individuals have a significant issue. For instance, you may wind up caught up in social media networking. You may end up investing a great deal of energy talking with companions. You may likewise be disturbed by TV shows and even music.

To keep away from these interruptions, you ought to put forth a valiant effort to have a decent workspace that is liberated from disturbances. You ought to likewise be sufficiently principled to diminish occasions of being stressed or distracted.

5 Must-Know Time Management Tips for Traders

Low maintenance dealers have it harsh. While we as a whole prefer to consider online markets trading nonstop as a colossal favorable position, it doesn't come without its obstructions. Because a market is open doesn't imply that the time you are available is a fitting time to trade. Nor does it constantly imply that one has sufficient opportunity to really break down the market in the way that it ought to be, and settle on proper choices dependent on the data consumed. The lucky opening for any low maintenance dealer is moderately little, and not many individuals adjust a trading reasoning around this while genuinely figuring out how to make it work.

Managing time is an enormous roadblock for some fire up dealers, as they are just not used to a fixed daily schedule, also experimentation/expectation to learn and adapt gets in the way of clean consistency.

Attached to risk, time is an issue that should take into account one's character type. Basically, if your character type searches for fast activity and for the most part comprises little patience at that point trading low maintenance will be such a lot harder thing to achieve.

Discovering transient opportunities consistently can be simple when you're spending the main part of the day on investigation. That being said, extremely high-likelihood trading dependent on your individual speculation system is, in many cases, rare all through the session. In this manner endeavoring to pack in a full trading session where you end level in 60 minutes or 3 hours with interruptions is heading off to all that a lot harder to sharpen in and center around what you truly need to.

Terrible traders will, in general, be brimming with gaps. Be that as it may, very frequently, those gaps are just inadequacies in information, both present and long haul. With an absence of time accessible, important data can without much of a stretch get skipped, putting the trader at an extreme hindrance.

Here are some quick tips that can conceivably guide you the correct way with regards to dealing with your time as a dealer:

1. Adjust your trading theory with your character type and the time you have accessible

I can't reveal to you the number of traders I witness endeavoring to trade a specific program that conflicts with each embodiment of who they truly are. Elements may meddle with their speculation on this issue, and time is surely one of them.

It is safe to say that you are the sort to show restraint? Is it safe to say that you are restless and can't keep still? If you will, in general, feel fidgety and are a part-time trader, at that point, you extremely just may have one alternative: adjust a transient technique that you can manage serenely in the time you have and compel yourself not to "try too hard." As such, take transient trades, however, don't over-strive regarding the number of sets you are exchanging. The appropriate examination requires some investment, and in the event that you are everywhere as far as what you can sensibly assimilate in during a solitary session, you are likely trying too hard.

In the event that you are a greater amount of the patient, orderly type, at that point, you are likely more qualified towards longer-term objectives. You may utilize the utilization of cutoff orders for execution or basically float in the method for longer-term specialized or principal plays. Stops and go out on limb benefits are large and risk is ordinarily a lot of lower. Individuals without a great deal of time on their plates may favor more extended term techniques as they're just not there to observe each tick, nor do they want to. Full-time dealers that longer-term utilization procedures are generally contributed over a scope of monetary standards, adding more enhancement to the pot (also keeping them occupied all through some random day).

Regardless of whether your character type takes into account a short, medium, or longer-term trading reasoning all depends. In any case, this ought to be stage one with stage two concentrating on fitting that way of thinking inside the limits of time that you have accessible.

2. Never sacrifice sound investigation

If there is one territory that you never need to hold back on is sound examination. Merchants that exclude pertinent pieces of data are truly doing simply aimlessly taking a look at an outline and making an uneducated supposition with respect to what will occur straightaway. Take the brief period that you have and assimilate yourself in investigation. In the event that you don't have the opportunity to think about the setting of all sets accessible, at that point, don't anticipate exchanging them. Sound investigation is basic. In the event that I glance back at any of my deplorable minutes as a trader, they, as a rule, happen essentially in light of the fact that I missed something little preceding execution. When I understand a slip-up was settled on, I would have no real option except to cut the string, a difficult exercise. Utilize your time carefully and possibly execute when your degree of certainty is exceptionally high.

3. Burrow deep and do it quick – maintain a strategic distance from the interruptions

Telephone ringing free, TV blasting out of sight, taking a look at general news sites, or YouTube are basically horrendous for your trading. Likewise, with some other work, they represent an immense interruption and are the snappiest method to get prevented from acquiring essential data that will do just help you as far as execution. Take the brief period that you have and basically dispose of interruptions that represent a danger to perfect, succinct and profound examination that is essentially required for your advancement. Close the door, shut out the clamor and pay attention.

4. Adjust to a methodical method to ingest data

You should commonly utilize a straight approach with regards to investigation with a significant accentuation on the association. Traders that are disorderly in their investigation or just navigate starting with one theme then onto the next will in general, end up dispersed or confounded.

Start with explicit, respectable news destinations: those that generally give me an "enormous picture" sees on current happenings. These are all at the front of my bookmarks and effectively available. "Fun" bookmarks are sorted independently and avoid the ones that issue most.

For a point of interest, you should, at that point, drill down into your intraday news channel action. Go ahead and check relationships and different markets so as to build up a balanced and widely inclusive information bank of the present circumstance. When you make a general assurance that you are happy with your insight into the world of that specific trade, you can start boring into outlines. Do the same straightforward investigation you have been doing for a considerable length of time, looking over numerous time spans and separating everything into littler segments.

While it does not have to be carefully "top-down", it still has to be organized. Start with a large scale picture and make endeavors to separate things into littler parts. Conventional top-down investigation has its inadequacies: on the off chance that you are making conclusions dependent on a full-scale view alone and that view isn't right, everything that follows is a wash and you might be setting yourself up for calamity. Remember a worldwide approach and understand that market timing is similarly as critical as some other part.

5. Try not to drive a window of time

Risk management rule #1: don't do anything by any stretch of the imagination. Straightforward? Indeed. Easily done? No.

In the event that you happen to lean toward a short window of time as far as normal trade length, you need to comprehend the consequences that accompany it: you will have days where you are basically not happy with any trade, paying little mind to the time you put resources into investigation. Experts are marketers and bend over backward to drive action down the throats of perusers each possibility they get (also most are specialists = you exchange, it is beneficial for them). The reality, be that as it may, is if you can't profit from what you know, you shouldn't do anything. You ought to appreciate trading and everything that accompanies it, so don't attempt to constrain something that simply isn't right.

Throughout time, I have seen a huge scope of trading methodologies that incorporate various windows of time. However, a trader shouldn't pick this way of thinking dependent on this factor alone. Spare time is something that is valuable to every one of us, however, utilizing it admirably and positive P&L is about the main thing that will enable us to have a greater amount of it. In a business where "timing is everything," dealing with your work process is similarly as essential as any arrangement of trade execution.

Chapter Five

Becoming a Great Stock Trader: Getting Started and Best Practices

Numerous individuals fantasize about profiting with stock trading, and others just marvel every once in a while in the event that it very well may be finished. A huge number of financial specialists make cash playing the business sectors consistently, and however the greatest additions are the most energizing and what stands out as truly newsworthy, there's a lot of subtlety and loads of moderate structure wins for stock traders. Figuring out how to make money trading stocks will require some serious energy; however, it is a reachable objective.

Stock trading is a risky movement. If you give it a shot, you'll have to anticipate misfortunes — a few organizations win, and some lose each day. In any case, with continuous research and a comprehension of which organizations merit putting resources into and why you can make money trading stocks.

Beginning as a Brand-New Stock Trader

Beginning and making money trading stocks are two unique things. In case you're new to the game, pursue these means to set yourself up for progress as you gain understanding:

- Research market patterns: Even the best brokers don't rest with regards to research. You have to find out about market inclines just as trustworthy sources where you can remain current on breaking news. "Kiplinger," "The Economist," and "Bloomberg" are a couple of trustworthy stock-trading magazines to add to your day by day understanding list. It's likewise worth after the web journals and web-based life records of industry specialists, including effective brokers, business analysts, and different experts.

- Create an account with a trading site: Once you're prepared to begin trading, you'll have to make a record with an exchanging site — a site like Scottrade, TradeKing, or TD Ameritrade. Prior to picking a help, read through client audits and BBB evaluations, if accessible, to affirm that the site is respectable. You'll additionally need to perceive what exchange expenses and different charges you'll pay for utilizing the administration. In the event that you need assistance narrowing down your decisions, search for benefits that will enable you to trade, for example, financial specialists examine instruments, portable applications, or client care administrations.

- Work on: Trading stocks isn't simply researched, and it's significantly something other than exchanging stocks. If you need to show signs of improvement and see an arrival on your ventures, you have to rehearse. Before you profit, create an account on a site like ScottradeELITE or OptionsHouse and profit. This will assist you with getting acquainted with how trades are set and what choices you'll make when a stock is doing ineffectively or well. This can assist you in figuring out how trading functions before utilizing genuine cash.

In case you're a new investor, you may be moving toward the market from a general point of view. This is incredible, yet after some time, you'll need to concentrate on a territory that you're a specialist in or love finding out about. The market is brimming with a great many alternatives, and it's difficult to bounce on each great exchange that travels every which way every day. It's basically better to concentrate on a little region of the market as you gain understanding as a dealer.

Fortunately, as another broker, you can inquire about and investigate uninhibitedly without adhering to a specialization immediately. Simply realize that sooner or later, you'll need to pick and ace a particular piece of the market. Likewise, in case you're a fledgling looking for a trading site, recollect that you don't need to pick one immediately. A few people create accounts with two or three sites and afterward thin their decisions later when they have a more clear comprehension of which pleasantries, administrations, and expenses are best for their trading technique.

Some Frequently Asked Questions

I'll address a portion of the more typical inquiries and remarks here:

- How would you pick the correct stocks?

This may sound more difficult than one might expect — all things considered, if everybody picked the correct stocks inevitably, there wouldn't be any misfortunes. In all actuality, the correct stock isn't generally the most outstanding or the most energizing. Prior to choosing to put resources into an organization, ask yourself these inquiries:

* How gainful is the organization? In case you're purchasing stock and need its value to build, you'll have to assess the organization's budgetary reports. These records are accessible online for any organization that is traded openly. In case you're experiencing difficulty discovering this data, you can contact the business to get a physical duplicate of the latest yearly report.

* Is the organization prone to be beneficial pushing ahead? Regardless of whether the yearly report didn't show any productivity, an organization may even now merit putting resources into. Check the business' initiative, its yearly costs, and its obligation. You can likewise survey its monetary records and salary explanations to evaluate whether the organization is probably going to be or remain beneficial later on. You may likewise discover, for instance, that another or low-benefit organization has as of late

obtained some veteran officials. This kind of progress is a convincing motivation to put resources into a business.

* What brought on any losses? On the off chance that you locate a poor quarterly exhibition in the money related report, it doesn't really imply that it's not worth putting resources into the organization. Research and reveal what added to this low execution, and solicit whether there's a hazard from a rehash. What's more, if there is a risk of another poor quarter, you'll have to choose whether the potential result merits contributing in any case.

* How has the organization done contrasted with its friends and industry? In the event that you go over a loss or gain, it's conceivable that variables identified with the business — not really the organization — added to these outcomes. Contrast the organization's stock history with its rivals to perceive how it has fared over the previous years. Likewise, see industry patterns. When stocks were up or down for the whole business, did the organization proceed true to expectations? Or, did the endeavor exceed expectations or pass up development that contending organizations delighted in?

As you gain understanding, you'll add your very own inquiries to this list so you can vet a stock and ensure it works for your trading procedure. You may likewise have criteria to advise when it may be satisfactory to veer off from your technique. This is the kind of subtlety that you can just create through broad research, practice, and genuine exchanging. For complete apprentices, however, it's prescribed to stay with surely understood organizations that have loads of information about their exchanging chronicles, initiative, and productivity. It's additionally a decent practice, to begin with only a limited quantity of cash.

Note that a few people likewise have rules about things like just trading with an unmistakable brand or an endeavor with long periods of accomplishment. Contingent upon how moderate or extreme you need to be as a broker, you may receive a portion of these techniques or relinquish them for different conditions, such as having a strong plan of action paying little mind to time in activity or offering a specific kind of item or administration.

- How would you purchase your first stock?

After you've investigated a few organizations and working on purchasing stocks for all intents and purposes for no particular reason (and experience), it's a great opportunity to attempt the genuine trade.

Sign on to your trading site account, and search for some well-investigated, dependable stocks.

It may be enticing, to begin with, something dangerous or contribute a major sum, yet it's ideal to consider making the plunge with a little exchange.

It's normal for amateurs to invest as meager as $1,000 while regardless they're learning.

Make sure to check for exchange expenses, however. Since you're currently working with an official record and exchanging genuine stocks, these sorts of charges will apply.

- Would you be able to Trade Stocks for a Living?

A great many individuals trade stocks as their all-day employment, and a great many others appreciate trading part time. How you approach stocks is totally up to you. You can make sense of how to make cash exchanging stocks at home, or you can seek after day trading as a profession.

A few people likewise appreciate trading all the more inactively through a mutual fund or working with a specialist to encourage trades. In a mutual fund, you arrange with a gathering of different financial specialists and pull your money together for contributing by an expert reserve supervisor. These investments are regularly expanded over an assortment of ventures and areas. Another decision is to join a stock trading group or online network where you can discover understanding and backing — which is surely significant for new traders.

- What Amount Can You Make From Stocks in a Month?

How much money you would be able to make from stocks relies upon your trading technique, your specialized area, how the business sectors are performing, and endless different elements.

Proficient, full-time traders can make over $5,000 in a month. The definite return rate likewise changes, relying upon the sum contributed. In case you're simply beginning or just trading on the low, you can even now make hundreds or thousands per month. In addition, as you gain expertise and reinvest your profit, you can procure substantially more on a month to month premise.

Tips for New Traders

New brokers have various techniques and logical strategies to research and attempt as they approach the market. Below are some tips to help.

1.) Take Out Time to Peruse Different Types of Markets, Strategies, and Analysis Methods

Traders with more experience can return to the procedures they use, as well, and check whether they can change their way to deal with start turning a benefit. These are only a couple of options you can seek after as a broker:

- Trading penny stocks: Penny stocks are low-esteem stocks traded for under $5 per share. The profits are commonly low, but at the same time, there's less hazard since you won't need to invest a great amount in beginning trading. It's additionally conceivable to make a tremendous benefit in trading these reasonable stocks. You'll need to find out about over the counter markets and put additional work into examining an organization's money related history since organizations that trade penny stock don't need to meet the severe monetary prerequisites of the New York Stock Exchange or NASDAQ.

- Day trading: As a day trader, you'll open and close a few trades inside the same session. Since these traders are taking a look at variances inside a little time span, they're scanning for various signs of a decent exchange than long haul investors. Day trading is commonly not advised for learner investors.

- Putting resources into long-and transient techniques: You would someday be able to trade, clutch stocks for a considerable length of time, or locate a stock methodology someplace in the middle. There's heaps of adaptability by the way you exchange, and individuals have made a benefit utilizing different systems, approaches, and procedures in the stock trade.

Notwithstanding investigating various kinds of trading or procedures that might be more qualified to your character or money related objectives, you can take a look at various market examination techniques to give you an edge or put you on track to benefit.

The essential examination techniques are fundamental and technical. Both are utilized to foresee value changes and consequently educate which stocks to purchase and when. The thing that matters is that a basic examination takes a gander at the organization — its initiative, benefit history, foreseen increases, future objectives, notoriety, and so on — to check the stock's worth.

A technical analysis, nonetheless, sees market patterns and what drives financial specialists to settle on stock choices. You may discover accomplishment by moving your concentration starting with one investigation technique then onto the next or by attempting a blend of the two to educate your trade decisions.

2.) Trade in Dividend Stocks or Initial Public Offerings

Another choice for turning a benefit as a broker is to put resources into high return profit stocks. With this kind of venture, the organization delivers investors profits — a percent of organization benefits — each quarter. Financial specialists get a profit paying little mind to whether their stock has acknowledged in value.

Beginning open contributions are another decision. These are the primary stocks an organization ever offers, and however, most new businesses come up short, it tends to be an awesome chance to get a stock at its least ever cost. Since the organization won't have earlier benefit information, however, you'll need to accomplish more research about elements like administration and the organization's field-tested strategy and course before deciding if the first sale of stock is a decent risk.

3.) Perfecting Your Trading Skills

89

You don't need to be a specialist to make money trading, yet as you place more ventures and continue rehearsing and inquiring about, you'll normally show signs of improvement at trading stocks. On the off chance that you find that you're reliably not profiting on your trading — paying little respect to whether you're another dealer or have some understanding — you can pursue these pointers to help make something happen.

4.) Follow Some Stock Trading Best Practices

On the off chance that you find that your trades aren't getting positive returns, return to the inquiries you pose to assist you with picking an organization to put resources into. You may need to include or change the criteria you use to pick organizations.

You can likewise attempt some other accepted procedures for profiting in online stock trading, for example, putting resources into mid-and enormous top organizations. The previous have a market capitalization between $2 billion and $10 billion, and the last has a market capitalization of over $10 billion. Putting resources into these organizations is regularly productive on the grounds that market capitalization means that the organization's stock value contrasted with its extraordinary offers.

Another choice is to add an additional progression to your due tirelessness when examining organizations: tuning in to an organization's profit telephone calls. In the event that you've just evaluated the organization's quarterly profit discharge, this extra advance will give you a more clear comprehension of the business' authority and plan for pushing ahead.

5.) Monitor the Markets Every Day

Individuals beginning their first day of trading and those who've been in the business for quite a long time share one significant duty regarding all intents and purpose: observing the business sectors consistently. This will assist you with remaining over creating patterns, but on the other hand, it's vital to the time tested exchanging mantra of purchasing low and selling high.

Regardless of whether you plan on being a traditionalist, forceful, present moment, or long haul merchant, this general guideline should control your contributing choices.

6.) Buy Low and Sell High

Purchasing low and selling high is anything but difficult to recall, and it's a demonstrated technique for mesh a benefit as a merchant. In any case, you would prefer not to settle on motivation choices at whatever point a stock value climbs or dips. Truth be told, it's imperative never to freeze when a stock dips under the value you paid since the sum may bounce back.

To choose whether a sum is high or low enough to warrant an exchange, do this:

- Take a look at the organization's income per offer and representatives' buy action.

- You likewise need to take a look at the business' administration, benefit history, and life span.

You need to purchase low. However, you likewise need to put resources into an organization that will recoup — ideally directly after you've gained their stock.

A similar guideline applies to selling high.

In the event that you need to sell the stock so you can reinvest the benefits, you need to ride the flood of the stock worth expanding for whatever length of time that conceivable. The organization's prosperity may likewise imply that the business can reinvest in itself, which may additionally drive share value.

Persistence is thus important, however, you additionally need to know when a value is probably going to level or decrease. Following industry patterns and experts' actions can assist you with pinpointing the best time to sell.

In case you're keen on day trading or short selling, purchasing low and selling high will be imperative to your prosperity. You'll additionally be generally intrigued by unpredictable markets since frequent increments and declines in stock worth open the entryway for frequent gainful trades. There are loads of intrinsic risks, however, in unstable markets.

7.) Diversify

In spite of the fact that you'll, in the long run, become a specialist in a specialty advertise, a great arrangement for seeing predictable additions is to expand your portfolio. This is just prescribed once you have a strong comprehension of how the market functions and how to purchase and sell stock.

Diversification is significant since it secures you against industry changes. For instance, if every one of your stocks were in tech and an administration guideline or new development contrarily influenced stock costs in that part, the entirety of your speculations would be affected. A various portfolio is insignificantly influenced by such patterns.

This methodology is likewise a decent method to adjust high-risk and preservationist ventures. Putting resources into new companies is commonly risky, for example, since most are covered inside five years. On the off chance that you've put resources into a built-up organization in a specific industry, however, you can purchase stock in a startup in a similar section.

Their shared gainfulness could be all-around useful for the business, or maybe the greater organization will procure the littler one — netting you a sizable benefit.

8.) Reinvest

It very well may be enticing to leave trading once you've made a benefit. Nonetheless, on the off chance that you need to prevail in the long haul, it's shrewd to reinvest your income into other stock or into something less productive, however okay with solid, long haul benefits, similar to reserve funds or retirement account.

In Closing: Learn by Doing

To a novice, picking stocks may appear as though finding an organization that is performing great or searching for a startup venture flaunting an amazing item or administration and putting resources into them. For sure, a large number of the best stockbrokers bounced on great chances and left with tremendous additions. In any case, these individuals didn't fall in reverse into these examples of overcoming adversity.

Master traders carry their insight into the market each day. They realize what patterns to look for, and they recognize what makes a decent trade or awful trade — and when it merits disrupting their own guidelines. Certainly, a few people do luck out trading stocks.

In the event that you need to move unhesitatingly realizing that you can make cash exchanging stocks, however, you'll always have to be taking a shot at your methodology, watching out for showcase patterns, and standing prepared to strike at the correct chance.

Regardless of whether you're absolutely new to trading or have been bringing about certain losses and need to make something happen, probably the ideal approaches to succeed and make money trading stocks is to watch what trades specialists make and figure out how they're computing their options.

The key is to comprehend why the trade is being made — regardless of whether a pro isn't trading a region you're acquainted with, on the off chance that you can contemplate their philosophy, you can apply their methods and way to deal with your own subject matter. Truth be told, this is the ideal approach to figure out how to make money trading stocks.

Conclusion

I believe congratulations are in order because you have made it to the end of this book, and you have been equipped with the knowledge you need for effective swing trading.

From what you have read, you would realize that the definitive objective of this book is to give you a superior chance to productively utilize the opportunities you encounter the same way a specialist trader would. Regardless of whether you are a regular broker that has lost a great deal of money before, this book will make trading quicker, simpler and multiple times increasingly productive for you.

And the sky is the limit from there!